here's

me

Elizabeth Butel

ETT IMPRINT

Exile Bay

For Angelica
Who was once a baby

Published by ETT Imprint, Exile Bay in 2020

First published by ABC Enterprises in 1991

ETT Imprint
PO Box R1906
Royal Exchange NSW 1225

ISBN 978-1-922384-44-7

Illustrated and designed by Janice Bowles

here's me

How to use this book

This book is for your baby, a month by month record of the first two years of life. You can use it in any way you like, to build up a picture that you and your child can later cherish-a storehouse of unique memories and sometimes vital information.

It will answer all those questions that your kids tend to puzzle over as they grow older. What was I like? What did I do? Where did I go? What did I see? You can write in it, draw in it, colour it in; and paste in photographs, birthday cards, wrapping paper, scraps of material, ticket stubs, newspaper cuttings and other odd mementos ... even the traditional lock of hair. Anything and everything that is important to you and your little one, that will one day recall the magic of those early times.

You can use it in a practical way too, as a reminder of immunization dates and baby clinic information-sleeping patterns, illnesses and all the tiny, but significant changes that are taking place.

Each drawing has a little space in which you can jot down what is happening in that month-developments, games, outings and other areas of interest. Our drawings are suggestions, things to get you thinking about what's important to you and your baby. If your little treasure is passionate about that old tin teapot then include it in the Favourite Toys section. You may not always want to *write* in the information; instead stick in a ticket stub from an outing or expedition, or a scrap of paper or material. There's no need to think too hard about it, just record your pleasure in your baby's growing personality and their excitement in discovering the world for themselves.

Keep a small box or bag handy to collect the photos and other odds and ends that will later mean so much. If there's an older brother or sister, big cousin or special friend, enlist their help with all the cutting and pasting. They'll think of things you've never even dreamed of. You don't have to do it month by month, but just use a spare evening every now and again to get things up-to-date.

Don't be afraid to cut up photographs into smaller pieces, or even snip a piece of fabric (no longer in use!) that your baby is fascinated by. And don't be afraid to paste over what you feel you don't need for that month, with a special photograph that sums it all up anyway. Use *Here's Me* like a scrapbook and have fun with it-it will be all the richer in the years to come.

Smiles, teeth, favourite toys, food, songs, nicknames, first sounds, first steps, first words, friends, pets, presents, birthdays, games and stories ... your baby, month by month!

DATE
EXPECTED

. . . .

. . . .

DATE
ARRIVED

. . . .

. . . .

BABY REFERENCE CARD

NAME_____

Birth Date__/__/__ Date of Discharge__/__/__   SEX_____

Birth Weight_____ kg._____ Cm.

Weight on Discharge_____ kg._____ Cm. (Clothed)

METHOD OF FEEDING ON DISCHARGE:

REMARKS:

GUTHRIE TEST

Bare Weight_____ kg._____ Cm.

Take this Card when making your first visit to your
Doctor or Baby Health Centre

mother's choice

. . . .

PERSONAL NOTICES

BIRTHS

THE NAME GAME

BOY   GIRL

GIRL   BOY

father's choice

. . . .

4

The Cast

mum ....

dad ....

baby ....

others ....

The Crew

midwife ....

doctor ....

others ....

....

The Bare Facts

weight ....

length ....

eyes like . . .

hands like . . .

nose like . . .

and . . .

The Big Gig

Starring

at

hospital, home or birth centre?

LABOUR BEGINS

LABOUR ENDS

Write in *your* details.
Add photos, cut-outs . . . anything!

Paste in a photo

Resemblances

Write in
your
details

hair like . . .

lips like . . .

ears like . . .

feet like . . .

frowns like . . .

9

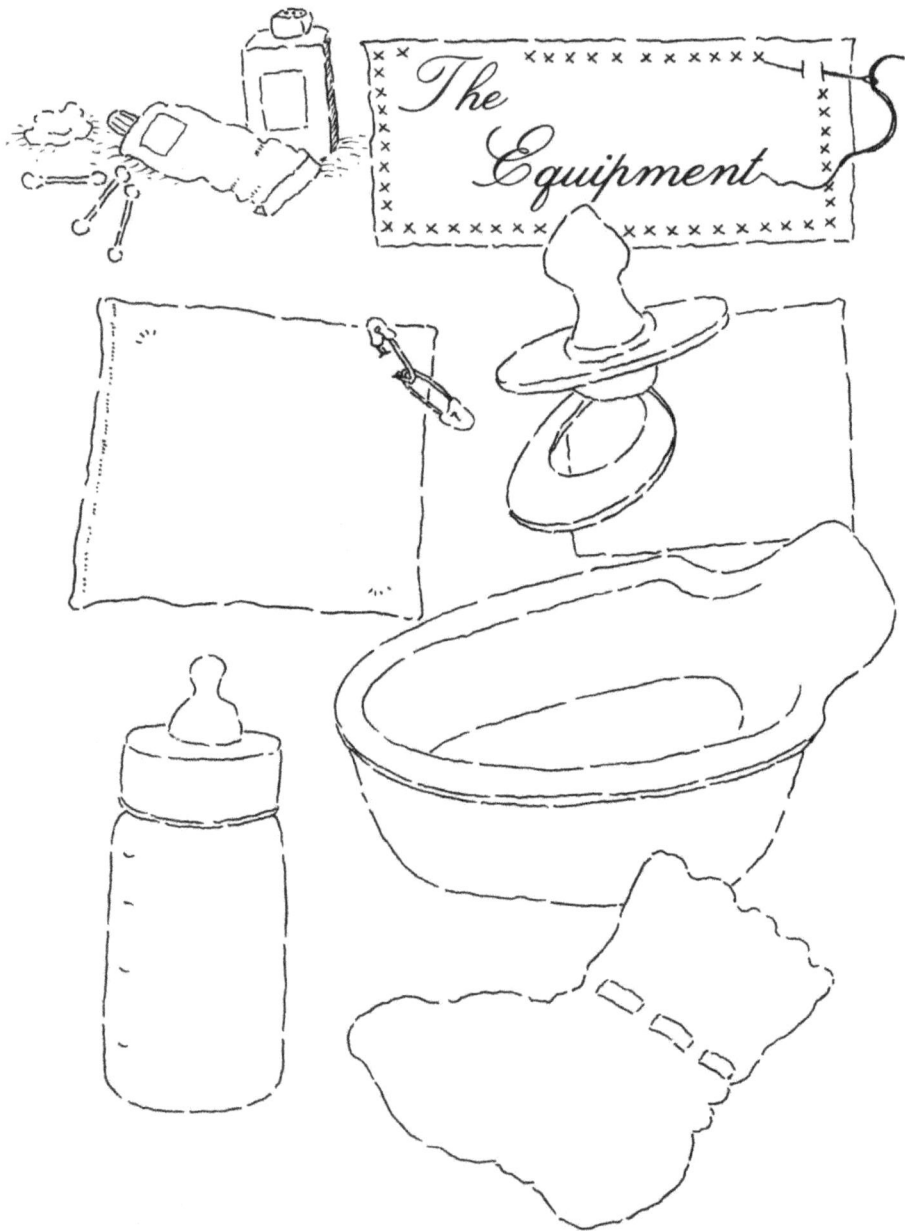

The Equipment

Write about the things your baby uses:

* where you got them
* who gave them to you
* what they look like
* any photos?

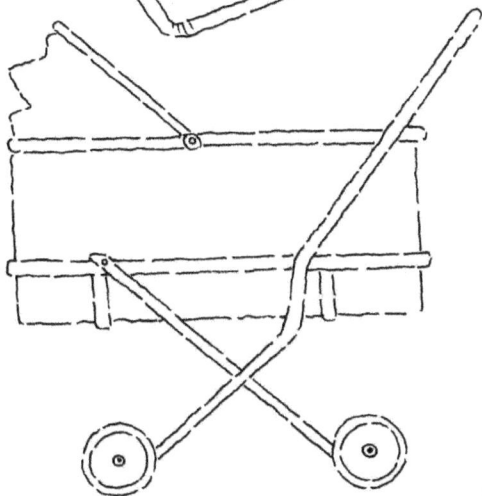

FiRST ToYS

Write about your baby's first toys:

* where you got them
* who gave them
* what they are
* any photos?

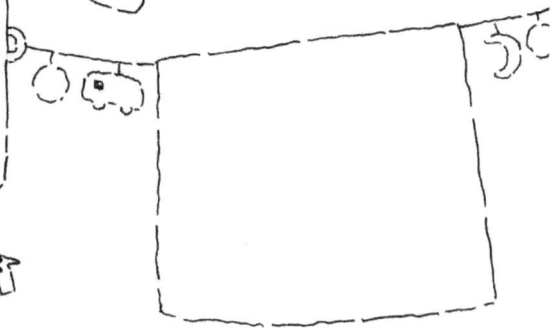

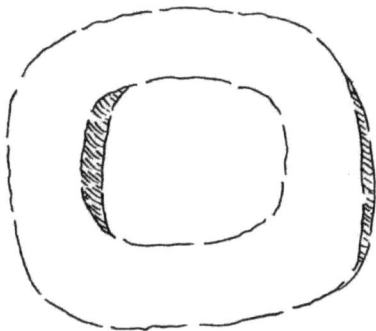

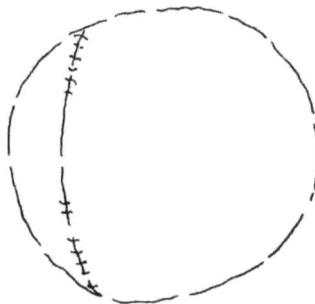

PRESENTS

sleeping pattern

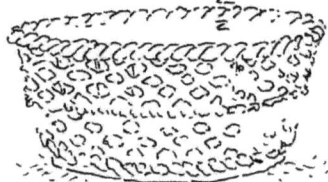

feeding pattern

....
....
....

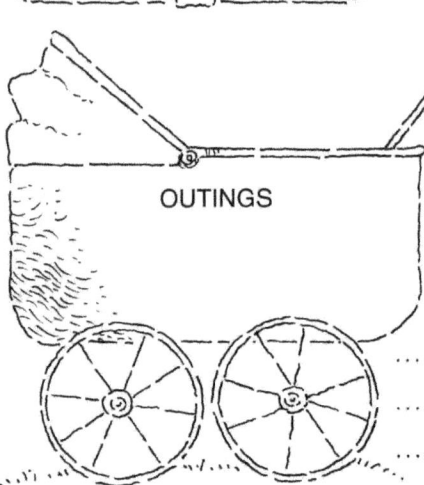

OUTINGS

OFF-COLOUR
MOMENTS

....
....
....

First Impressions

NICKNAME

VISITORS

and . . .

....
....
....
....
....
....
....

.

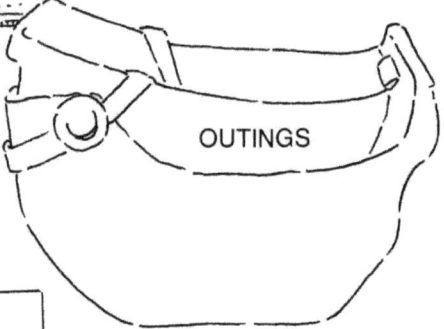

OUTINGS

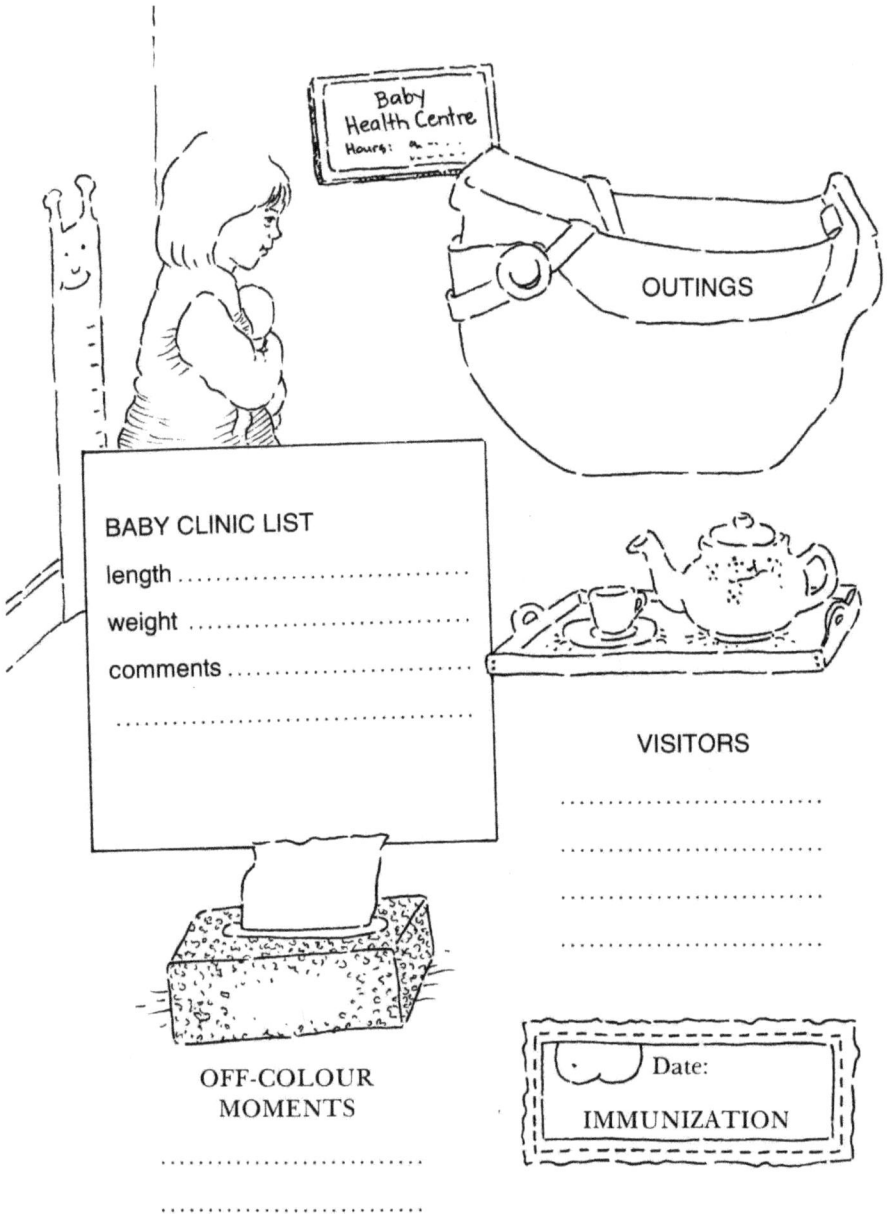

BABY CLINIC LIST

length ....

weight ....

comments ....

....

VISITORS

....

....

....

....

OFF-COLOUR
MOMENTS

....

....

Date:

IMMUNIZATION

When you're *smiling*

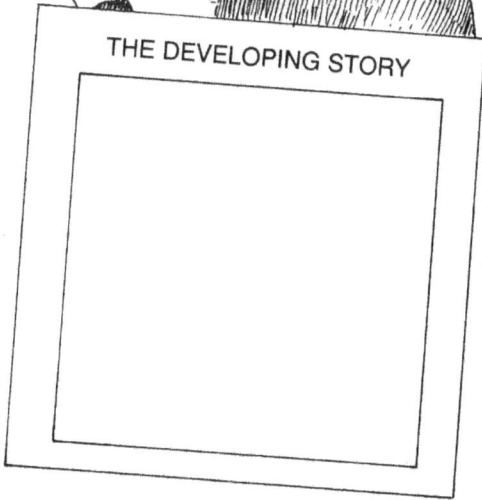

THE DEVELOPING STORY

feeding pattern

sleeping pattern

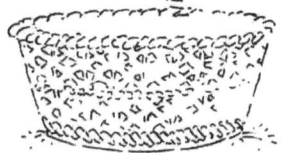

and . . .

2nd month

THE DEVELOPING STORY

sleeping pattern

OFF-COLOUR MOMENTS

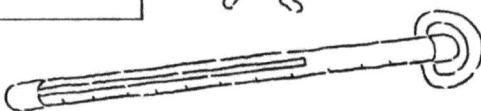

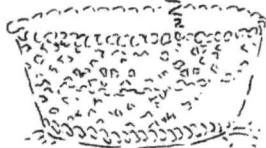

VISITORS

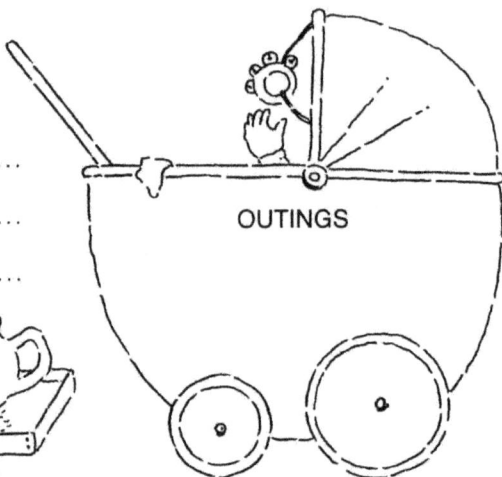

OUTINGS

Write in *your* details.
Add photos, cut-outs . . . anything!

The all-day sucker

FAVOURITE TOYS

sights and sounds

GAMES

feeding pattern

....
....
....

and . . .

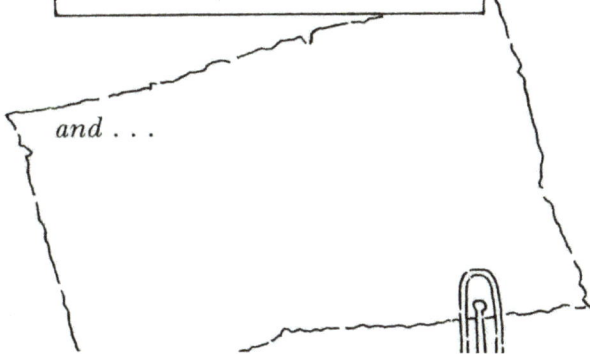

THE DEVELOPING STORY

sights and sounds

and . . .

sights

Shake, rattle and roll

GAMES

FAVOURITE TOYS

OFF-COLOUR MOMENTS

....
....
....

Date:

IMMUNIZATION

4th month

FAVOURITE
TOYS

THE DEVELOPING STORY

THE
TOOTH FAIRY

....
....
....

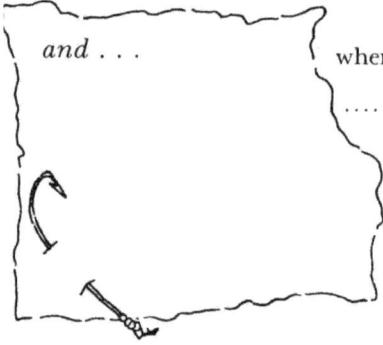

and . . .

where ....
....

when ....
....

OUTINGS

Bath Time

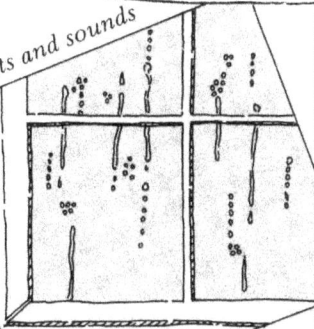

sights and sounds

GAMES

OFF-COLOUR
MOMENTS

....

....

....

5th month

FOOD,

THE DEVELOPING STORY

FAVOURITE TOYS

....
....
....

OUTINGS

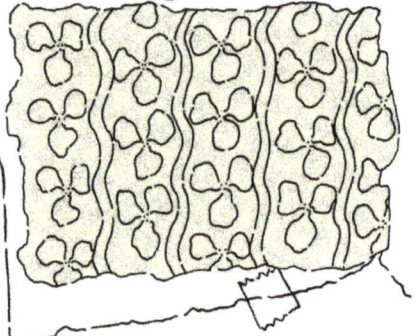

sights and sounds

and . . .

GLORIOUS FOOD

IMMUNIZATION

Date:

BABY CLINIC VISIT

length ....

weight ....

comments ....

....

THE
TOOTH FAIRY

where ....
....
when ....
....

OFF-
COLOUR
MOMENTS

NICKNAME

GAMES

6th
month

Washing
Daze

OUTINGS

GAMES

THE
TOOTH FAIRY

where ....

when ....

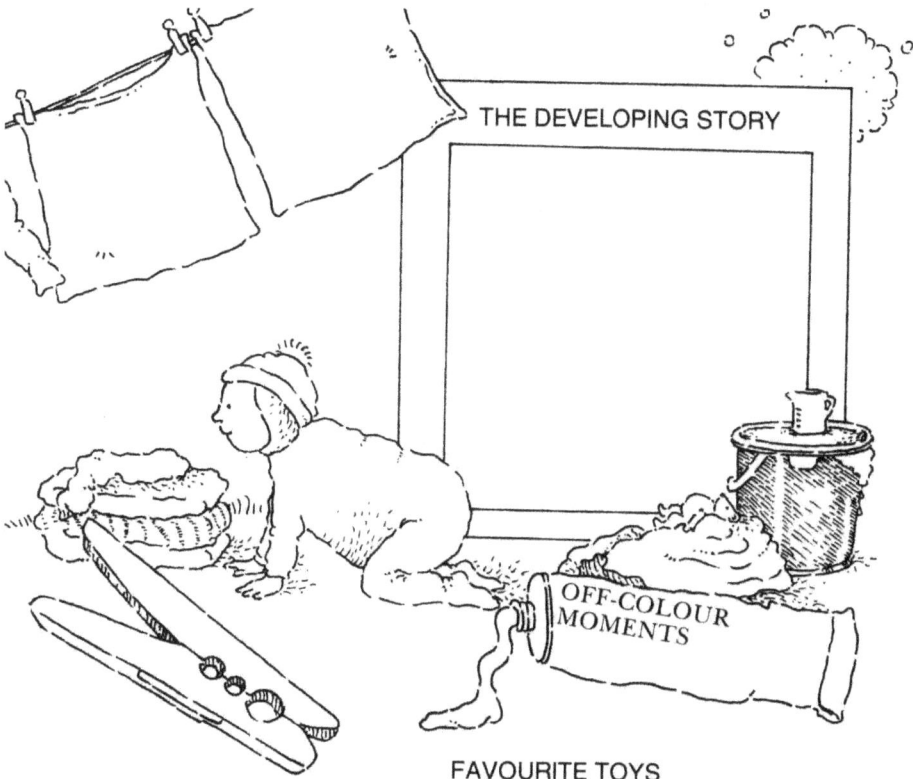

THE DEVELOPING STORY

OFF-COLOUR
MOMENTS

FAVOURITE TOYS

....
....
....

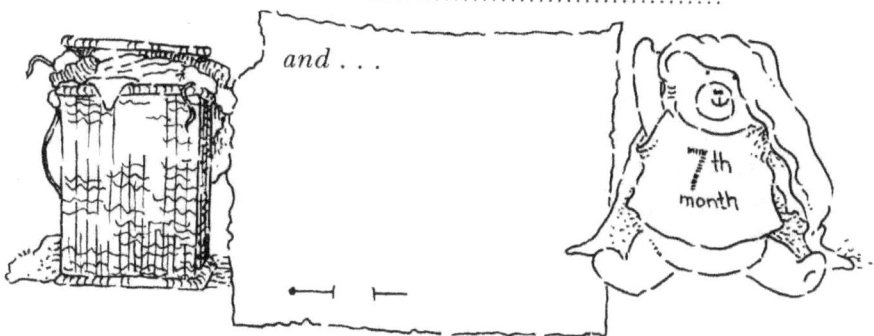

and . . .

7th
month

OUTINGS

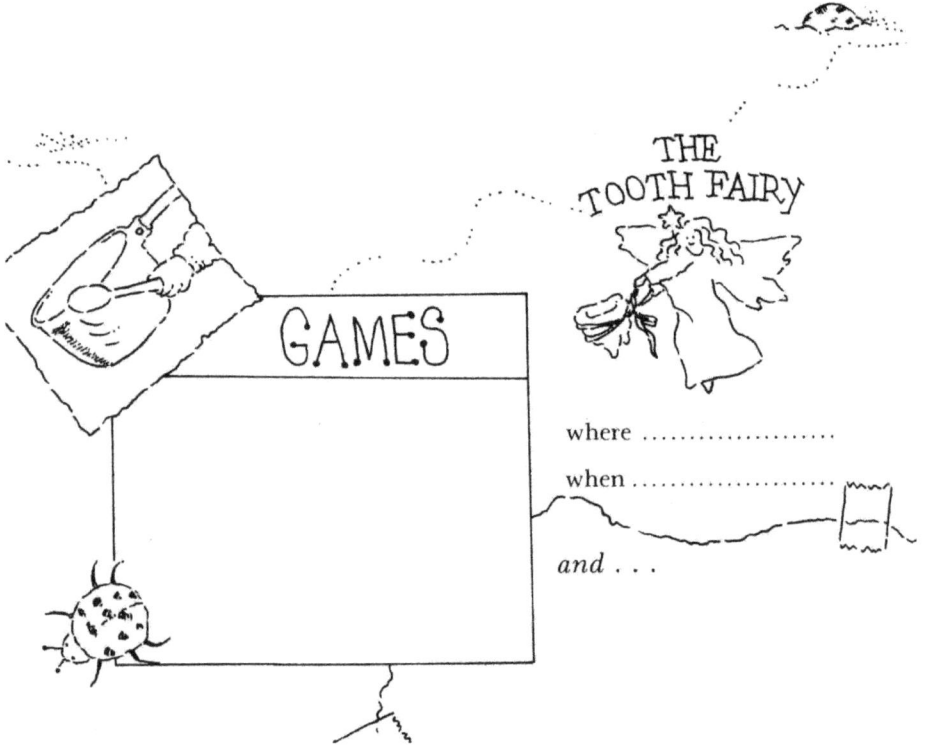

THE TOOTH FAIRY

GAMES

where ....

when ....

and . . .

Slip, Slip, Sliding Along

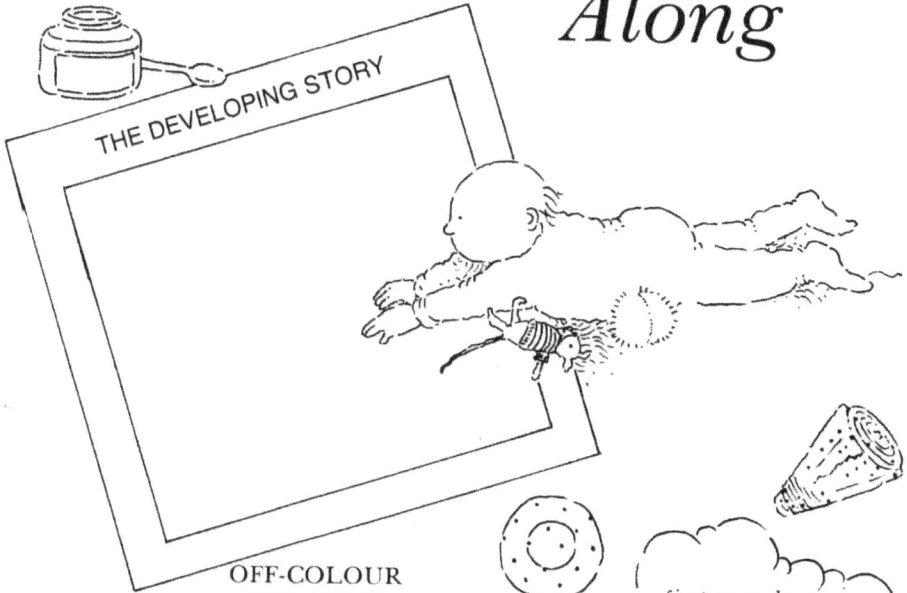

THE DEVELOPING STORY

OFF-COLOUR
MOMENTS

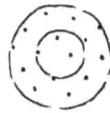

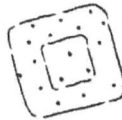

first sounds

FAVOURITE TOYS

Write in *your* details.
Add photos, cut-outs . . . anything!

8th
month

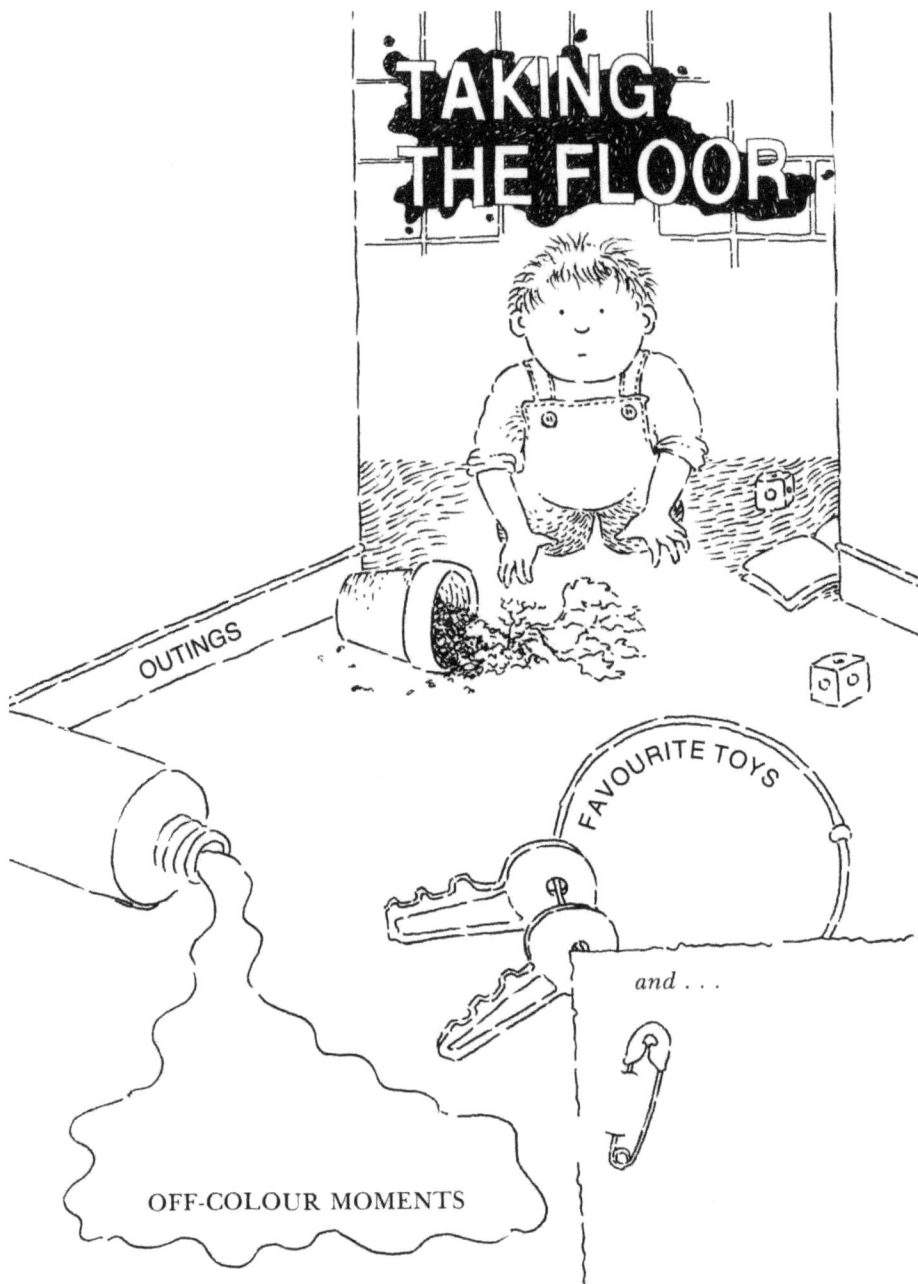

TAKING THE FLOOR

OUTINGS

FAVOURITE TOYS

and . . .

OFF-COLOUR MOMENTS

THE TOOTH FAIRY

THE DEVELOPING STORY

where ....

when ....

first sounds

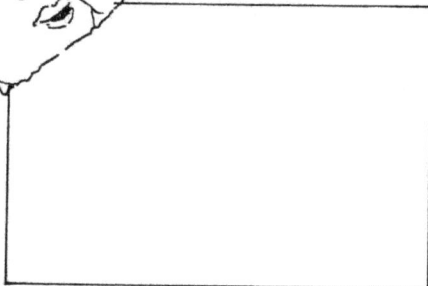

GAMES

9th month

OUTINGS

GAMES

OFF-COLOUR
MOMENTS

....
....
....

FAVOURITE TOYS

HOUSE KEEPING

THE DEVELOPING STORY

THE
TOOTH FAIRY

first sounds

where ....

when ....

and . . .

10th
month

first sounds

and ...

OUTINGS

GAMES

THE
TOOTH FAIRY

where ....

when ....

CRUISING

THE DEVELOPING STORY

OFF-COLOUR MOMENTS

FAVOURITE TOYS

11th mo

GARDENING

and . . .

THE
TOOTH FAIRY

where . . . .

. . . .

when . . . .

. . . .

first sounds

THE DEVELOPING STORY

OFF-COLOUR
MOMENTS

. . . .

. . . .

. . . .

GAMES

FAVOURITE TOYS

BABY CLINIC VISIT

length ....

weight ....

comments ....

....

NICKNAME

12th month

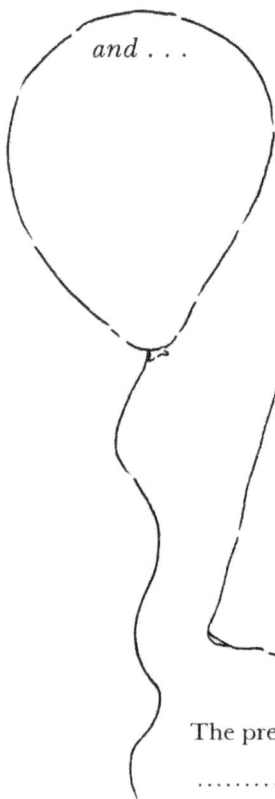

and . . .

The cake ....

....

....

The food

The presents ....

....

....

....

....

HAPPY BIRTHDAY
one year old!

THE PARTY

date:

time:

place:

The guests

Bedtimes

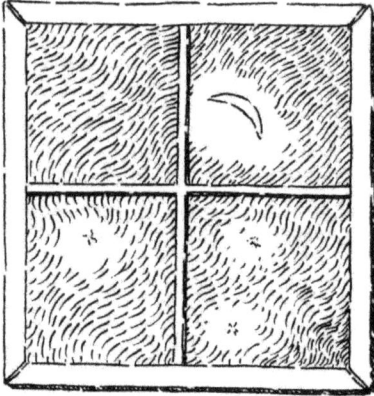

OUTINGS

new sounds

THE DEVELOPING STORY

Write in *your* details.
Add photos, cut-outs . . . anything!

GAMES

OFF-COLOUR MOMENTS

THE
TOOTH FAIRY

and . . .

....
.... where ....
.... when ....

FAVOURITE TOYS

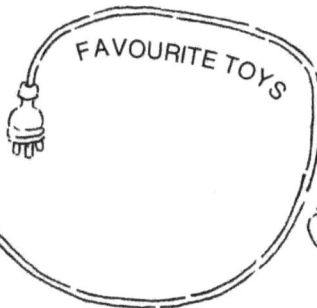

13th
month

Expeditions

GAMES

and . . .

The Sandman

THE DEVELOPING STORY

OFF-COLOUR MOMENTS

....
....
....

new sounds

THE TOOTH FAIRY

where ....
....
when ....
....

THE DEVELOPING STORY

THE TOOTH FAIRY

where ....

when ....

new sounds

FAVOURITE TOYS

and . . .

OFF-COLOUR MOMENTS

....
....
....

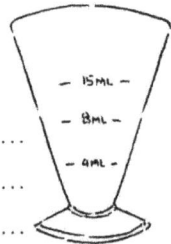

THE BABY BOOKWORM

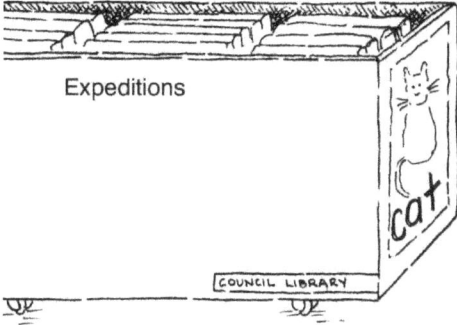

Expeditions

cat

COUNCIL LIBRARY

Date:

IMMUNIZATION

GAMES

15 month

INSIDE

OFF-COLOUR
MOMENTS

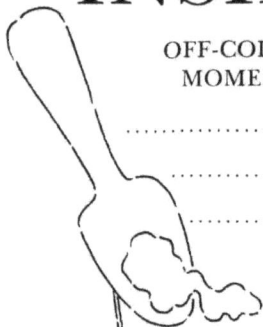

....

....

....

UP

USE NO
HOOKS

new sounds

GAMES

FAVOURITE
TOYS

....

....

and . . .

OUTSIDE

Expeditions

THE
TOOTH FAIRY

THE DEVELOPING STORY

where ....
....
when ....
....

16th
month

Making Mud

GAMES

PLAY GROUP

Joshua

OFF-COLOUR
MOMENTS

. . . .
. . . .
. . . .

Expeditions

Write in *your* details.
Add photos, cut-outs . . . anything!

Pies

THE
TOOTH FAIRY

where ....

when ....

THE DEVELOPING STORY

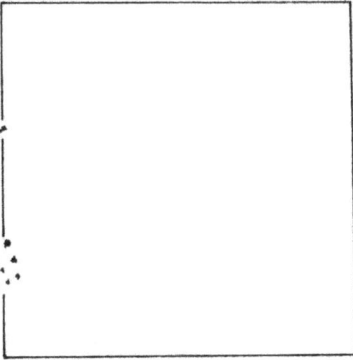

FAVOURITE TOYS

....

....

new sounds

and ...

17th
month

Rubber

BABY CLINIC VISIT

length ....

weight ....

comments ....

....

GAMES

FAVOURITE TOYS

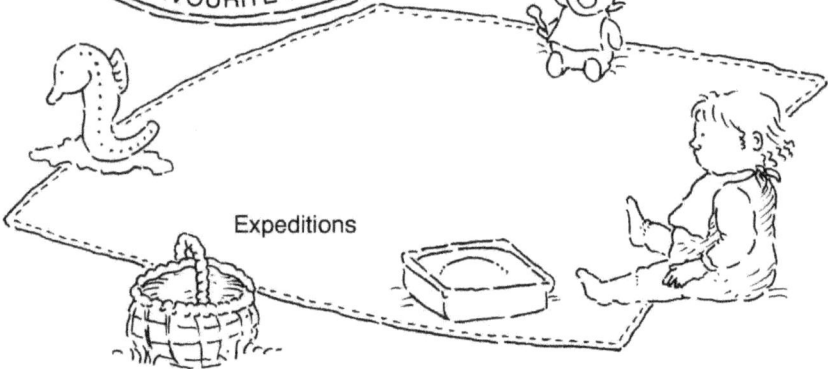

Expeditions

Duckie

and . . .

THE DEVELOPING STORY

THE TOOTH FAIRY

where ....
....
when ....
....

NICKNAME

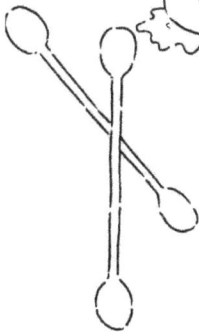

....
....
....
OFF-COLOUR MOMENTS

18th month

Animal Attraction

THE DEVELOPING STORY

and . . .

FAVOURITE TOYS

....
....

THE TOOTH FAIRY

GAMES

where ....
....
when ....
....

Expeditions

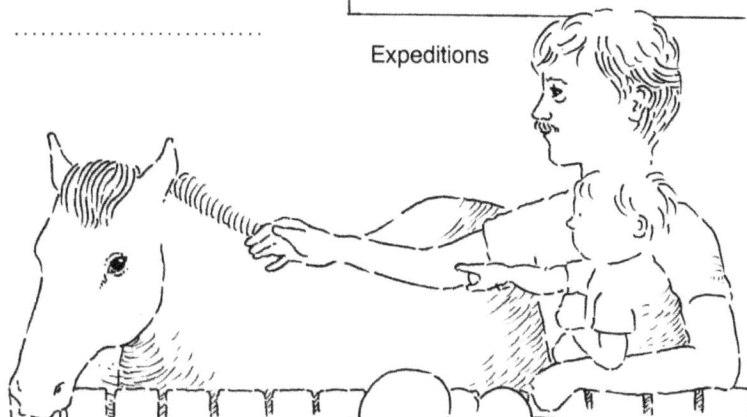

new sounds

....
....
....

OFF-COLOUR MOMENTS

Kitchen

THE DEVELOPING STORY

THE TOOTH FAIRY

where ....

when ....

OFF-COLOUR
MOMENTS

....
....
....

and . . .

Whizz

new sounds

GAMES

FAVOURITE TOYS

Expeditions

20th

The Park

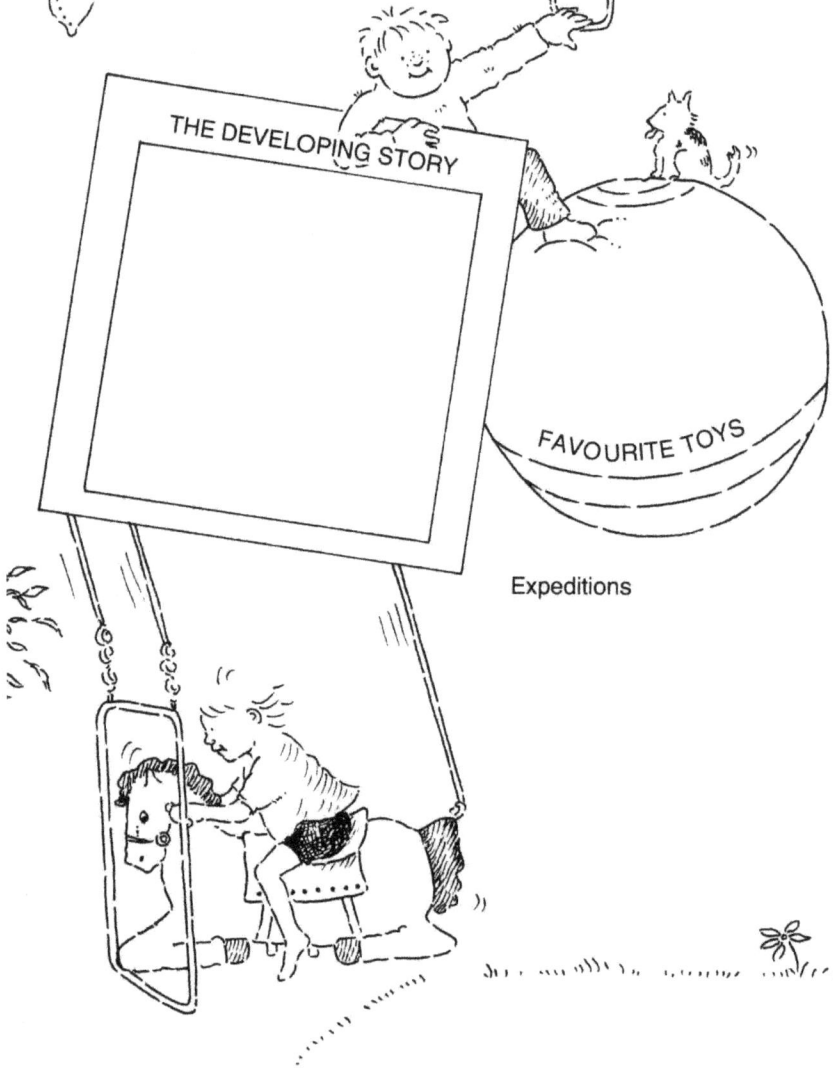

THE DEVELOPING STORY

FAVOURITE TOYS

Expeditions

Ranger

THE TOOTH FAIRY

GAMES

where ....

when ....

new sounds

and . . .

OFF-COLOUR
MOMENTS

....

....

....

21st
month

THE ENGINEER AN

OFF-COLOUR
MOMENTS

....

....

....

THE DEVELOPING STORY

and . . .

Expeditions

Write in *your* details.
Add photos, cut-outs . . . anything!

D THE *electrician*

FAVOURITE TOYS

new sounds

THE
TOOTH FAIRY

where ....
....
when ....
....

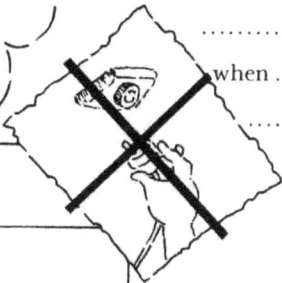

GAMES

22nd
month

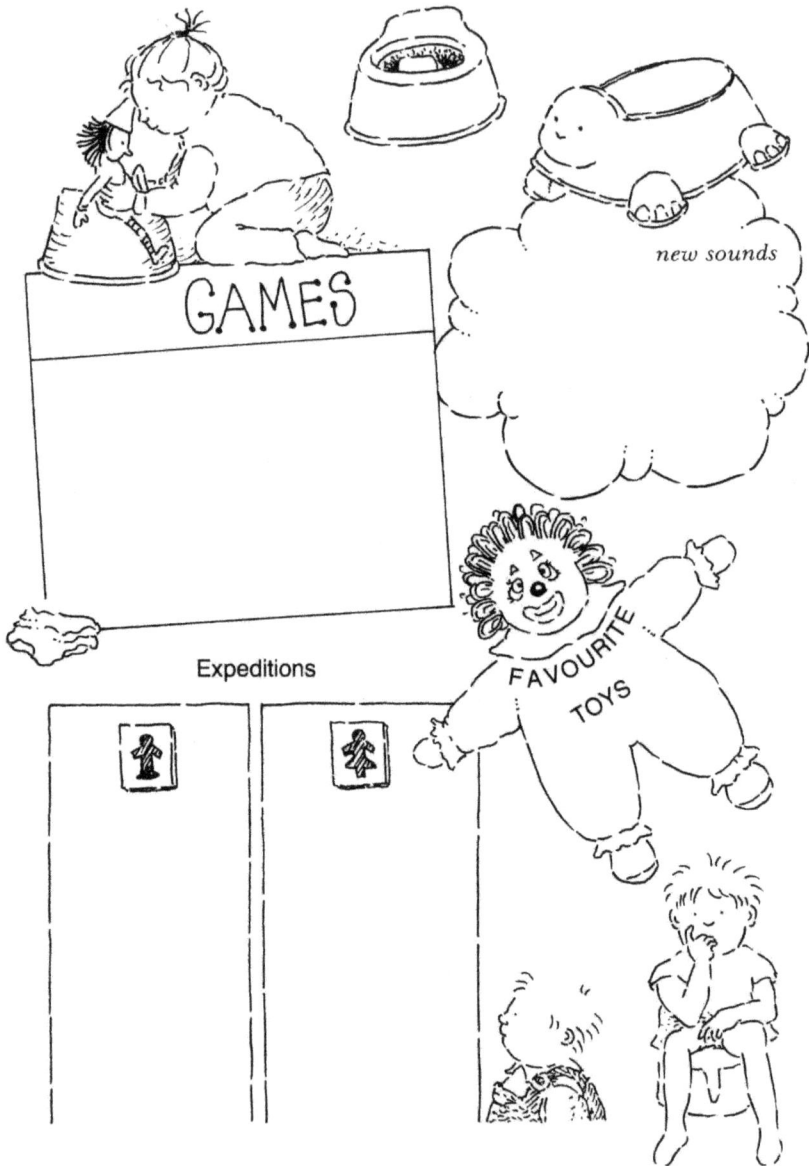

GAMES

new sounds

Expeditions

FAVOURITE TOYS

GOING POTTY

THE TOOTH FAIRY

where ....

when ....

THE DEVELOPING STORY

and . . .

OFF-COLOUR MOMENTS

23rd month

WHEELS

THE DEVELOPING STORY

and . . .

Expeditions

THE
TOOTH FAIRY

where ....

when ....

new sounds

OFF-COLOUR MOMENTS

....

....

....

GAMES

FAVOURITE TOYS

BABY CLINIC VISIT

length ....

weight ....

comments ....

....

NICKNAME

24th month

63

The presents

The guests ....

....

....

....

....

....

....

....

SECOND BIRTHDAY

2 PARTY

2   2   2

The cake:

The food ....
....
....
....

date:

place: